Washington Avenue Branch
Albany Public Libra
JAN

W9-DBT-151

TAILS from History

The Cat Who Ruled the Town

By May Nakamura

Illustrated by Rachel Sanson

Ready-to-Read

Simon Spotlight

New York   London   Toronto   Sydney   New Delhi

SIMON SPOTLIGHT
An imprint of Simon & Schuster Children's Publishing Division
1230 Avenue of the Americas, New York, New York 10020
This Simon Spotlight edition January 2019
Text copyright © 2019 by Simon & Schuster, Inc.
Illustrations copyright © 2019 by Rachel Sanson
All rights reserved, including the right of reproduction in whole or in part in any form.
SIMON SPOTLIGHT, READY-TO-READ, and colophon are registered trademarks of Simon & Schuster, Inc.
For information about special discounts for bulk purchases, please contact Simon & Schuster Special
Sales at 1-866-506-1949 or business@simonandschuster.com.
Manufactured in the United States of America 1218 LAK
10 9 8 7 6 5 4 3 2 1
Library of Congress Cataloging-in-Publication Data
Names: Nakamura, May, author. | Sanson, Rachel, illustrator. Title: The cat who ruled the town
by May Nakamura ; illustrated by Rachel Sanson. Description: Simon Spotlight edition.
New York : Simon Spotlight, 2019. | Series: Tails from history | Audience: Age 5-7.
Identifiers: LCCN 2018043070 | ISBN 9781534436435 (hardcover) | ISBN 9781534436428 (paperback)
ISBN 9781534436442 (ebook) Subjects: LCSH: Cats—Alaska—Talkeetna—Biography—Juvenile literature.
Classification: LCC SF445.5 .N35 2018 | DDC 636.80092/9—dc23
LC record available at https://lccn.loc.gov/2018043070

There is a small town in Alaska
called Talkeetna
(say: tall-KEET-nuh).
The town is so small that
fewer than nine hundred people
live there.

Most visitors pass through
Talkeetna on their way to Denali
(say: deh-NAH-lee).
Denali is the highest mountain peak
in North America.

But people also used to visit Talkeetna for another reason. They wanted to meet the mayor. Why was the mayor so special?

The mayor was a cat!

Stubbs the cat lived at
Nagley's Store.
His name was Stubbs
because he had a very short tail.

People in the town like to tell the story that in 1997, Talkeetna held an election to choose a town mayor.

The Talkeetna townspeople
didn't want to vote for anyone
on the ballot.
So instead they voted for Stubbs,
and he won the election!

The story is just a legend.
The town is actually too small
to have a mayor and a government.
But that didn't stop people
from calling Stubbs "the mayor"!

As an honorary mayor,
Stubbs lived a very nice life.
Every afternoon
Stubbs took a break
by drinking water
from a fancy glass.

Then he sat in the store
and waited for visitors.
People from all around the world
came to the store to meet Stubbs.
Some people pretended to have
an appointment with the mayor!

Stubbs greeted these visitors
by crawling onto their laps
and posing for pictures.

When he got tired,
he curled up into a ball
and took a long nap.

Stubbs liked to walk around town.
He visited local restaurants,
art stores, and bakeries
to say hello to the townspeople.

The walks made Stubbs sleepy, so he would take another nap. Wherever he slept, Stubbs always left a lot of fur to clean up!

Sometimes Stubbs went to the park.
The neighborhood kids loved petting
and playing games with Stubbs.
It was great to be the town mayor!

As the years passed,
Stubbs got older.
On many days he felt too tired
to greet visitors at the store.
Stubbs had been mayor
for nineteen years.
People wondered if he would retire.

Then one summer day in 2016,
Stubbs's owners had a surprise.
"Say hello to Aurora and Denali,"
they said.
"These cats are moving in
with all of us!"

Aurora and Denali had big blue eyes
and gray and white fur.
They were barely two months old.

Stubbs had never lived
with other cats before.
He stood away and growled.

The kittens loved to play.
They tumbled, jumped,
and ran up and down the stairs.
"Meow!" said Aurora.
"Meow!" said Denali.
Stubbs hissed.

But Aurora and Denali loved Stubbs.
They liked to follow him around
and sleep in the same bed.

As time went on,
Stubbs grew to love
the little kittens.
Aurora and Denali were the
newest members of the family
and of Talkeetna!

The three cats became close friends.
Aurora and Denali tumbled together
while Stubbs swatted playfully at
them. When they got tired,
they all curled up
and napped together.

Sometimes the two kittens joined
Stubbs at his mayoral work.
Aurora wasn't interested in meeting
all the visitors.
She didn't like to be petted.

But Denali, like Stubbs,
was great with visitors.
He loved all the attention.
He meowed, crawled onto laps,
and posed for pictures.

"Denali might become a good mayor
when he grows up!"
the people of Talkeetna
would often say.

Stubbs was happy to have new friends.

But most of all, Stubbs was happy to be loved by the people of Talkeetna . . . and the world!

· Facts About Alaska ·

- On January 3, 1959, Alaska was the forty-ninth state to become part of the United States.
- Alaska is the biggest state in the United States. It is bigger than the next three largest states—Texas, California, and Montana—combined. In terms of population, though, Alaska is the third smallest state!
- Denali, the highest mountain peak in North America, is 20,310 feet tall.
- More than ten thousand years ago, Russia and Alaska were connected by land. The Pacific Ocean separates them today.
- Alaska is the most northern state in the US. The coldest temperature ever recorded in Alaska was -80 degrees Fahrenheit in 1971. It was also the coldest temperature ever recorded in the United States!

· Facts About Cats ·

- Ancient Egyptians thought cats were magical and brought good luck. They even mummified the cats when they died!
- Cats usually have eighteen claws between their front and back paws. They retract their claws when they aren't using them.
- Cats are nocturnal, which means they are most active at night.
- Cats have great hearing. A human only has six muscles in each ear, but a cat has about thirty muscles!
- In 2016 there were almost eighty-six million pet cats in America!